Ho'

D

Your Clients

Copyright

ISBN: 9781549518515

Dedicated to...

All the salespeople of the world.

It's a tough gig,

but if you can do it

you absolutely should.

Contents

Intro

Over the last decade, I've been on a lot of sales training. I've completed courses and attended lectures; memorised models and lists of killer questions. I've been subjected to best practice, monthly conference calls and top tip PowerPoints. Despite all the variations and layers of complexity, it usually breaks down to the following:

1. Intro/Build Rapport
2. Question
3. Sell
4. Close

That's as basic as it gets. But here's the issue – 'build rapport' is thrown in there like it's the simplest thing in the world. Sometimes it's not even mentioned, and just assumed your clients will warm to you as soon as you declare your name and company. From experience, the opposite is more likely. If it were that easy, we'd all be best friends with our clients, and have instant, delightfully profitable business relationships.

Steps 2, 3 and 4 are given masses of attention, hours of focus and course content dedicated to "question funnels" and "needs based selling" and an arsenal of certified closes. However, if you don't make it past the intro - if your client doesn't like you enough to hear what's coming next - it's game over. Client X has disengaged and you're onto the next name on your hit list.

Very few of us in sales have the luxury of selling a product or service that is unique. We're rarely in a position to sit back, and watch our clients form an orderly queue to sign contracts. We must compete - for attention, opportunity and ultimately, business. Our livelihoods depend on it.

In a university lecture years ago I was told,

"The essence of sales is buying something for a fair price, from someone you like."

We're not pricing analysts but the "someone you like" part is where we can all influence our own success. If you can master that part of the sales process, it's a game changer. If your clients like you first, they will listen to what you say next, and ultimately, you'll create endless opportunities to sell.

Clients don't buy from salespeople they don't like. No one is desperate enough to use you when there are hundreds of other suppliers they'd rather deal with over you.

So, it got me thinking - where can us salespeople find the resources we badly need to get our clients to like us? What field of thought may have the valuable insights to enhance our sales game and give our likeability prowess the education it needs? And then it hit me.

The world of dating.

As someone who has done a fair bit of (field based) research in this arena, I can confirm that sales and dating go hand in hand. Both involve people at opposite sides of the equation, both have the sole aim of getting someone to like you, and both have great pay offs if you're able to nail your prospects.

In this book, you'll find tried and tested dating techniques that have the power to elevate your sales pitch and transform the way you approach your clients. Your likeability will become your competitive edge and your relationships with your clients will evolve past what you've been trained to aim for before.

I've been sales side for most of my career, client side more recently, and dating all the way through, so I can confidently say the chapters that follow give authentic, realistic and effective advice. You'll find a lot of **In real life** examples of how this works in practice, and the occasional **Date night** story to keep you interested.

And so, we begin.

Chapter 1 – Don't be a sales sleaze

How many times on a night out do you see some poor soul pestered by a chancer, who thinks they deserve a drink/dance/date just for turning up? In sales, we have an equivalent - the repeat offenders who hassle their clients with pesky, superficial, hard sells. These people are sales sleazes. And sleazy isn't a good look in sales or in life.

There may be a flaw in the way we are trained. Some companies actively promote the hard sell, the overdose of communication and the mindset that encourages "get rich or die trying" behaviour. However, grabby and assumptive is a huge turn off for your clients. No one owes you their business so don't act like your prospects are obliged to use you. It makes for a distasteful first impression and is a big contributing factor to the stereotype that all salespeople are cut throat, money hungry sharks.

Similarly, the egotistical view that your client is somehow missing out if they don't give you a shot, doesn't make them want you more. Playing the "it's your loss" card is risky, even more so when your client isn't that bothered about you to begin with. Clients usually have multiple options when it comes to who they work with, so get these attitudes out your head, as chances are they will survive just fine without you.

Date night

I went on a date once with a guy who I can only describe as a human octopus. It was a first date and I was being pleasant and tentative as always. But this chap just

latched right on from the word go; wrapped around me
(physically) at dinner to the point I could barely untangle
my own arm to put pizza in my mouth. In the taxi ride
home (separate homes) he even clambered into the
middle seat to be closer to me. Too much, yes?

As a client, I've experienced the same mannerisms from sales suitors. A salesperson who we were relatively open to doing business with, put us off by being so full on in the early stages of the relationship. Hard sells on the phone, up to 4 calls a day, a string of follow up emails and a worryingly strained voicemail. In a romantic setting, this person would be branded a stalker. So why do we think this is acceptable in sales? When I raised that it was too much heavy contact, I got a flippant email back, retorting, "Well you know what us sales guys are like!" It might as well have come with a winky face. That was the last time we dealt with them.

It's understandable why this can happen. Our interpretation of sales has a lot to do with how we were groomed. It might be what you were told to do, targeted to do, or what everyone in the office believes works. You may have to give the impression you bled trying to convince a client to use you if you're going to face your manager unscathed. You may just need that final deal to hit your bonus threshold, or dodge a performance review.

But please, make a mental note of how many times this method gets results. There might be a few quick wins if you were lucky, but was it the foundation of a long-lasting relationship? Did that client turn to you time and time

again, or did they just give you a one off as they couldn't
be bothered arguing?

In real life

*One of my old managers used to whisper the phrase
"softly softly catchee monkey" in my ear when I was
approaching potential customers on the sales floor. It was
annoying at first, as I was 17 and thought it was a Jungle
Book reference. But soon I discovered it's a viable sales
mentality. I was working in retail and had no appreciation
for a soft sell. I used to pounce on prospective customers
as soon as they were in a 10 metre proximity – the way I
was trained. I'd march swiftly up to them and launch into
my perfectly memorised sales speech. I would watch the
enthusiasm drain from their faces as they'd mumble
something about "just looking" and sidle away.*

The other symptom of sales sleazes is they can be passive
aggressive (sometimes not passive at all) when faced with
rejection. They're the type to bark "OK BYE" before
hanging up the phone* when they sense they're not going
to get what they want. Talk about leaving a sour taste in
your prospective client's mouth? Sure, they weren't going
to use you anyway you say, but they may tell their
colleagues, industry peers or god forbid, social media, of
your unsavoury behaviour.

*Whether it's during a fight with a partner or in a work
environment - if you've ever been hung up on, you'll
know it's the most infuriating thing someone can do. It
leaves you fighting the urge to fling the phone across the
room. For the first time in 10 years, I was hung up on by a
salesperson when I couldn't give them the information

they wanted. I was absolutely stunned, incensed, and let me tell you - they will be on my blacklist for life. Hanging up a little sharper than you should may be a small, impulsive act, but it's a sure-fire way to lose clients and have them swearing blindly that they'll never work with you or your company.

You'll start to see a trend emerge throughout this book and it's mainly to do with acting like a nice human being. People like dating nice humans. Clients also like working with them. And I'm by no means implying that those who work in sales are not nice people (mainly because I'm one of them) but it's important to notice that certain methods and behaviours are more accepted in sales culture than they would be in real life. Sometimes bad or out-dated practices have passed down through generations of managers and staff, and you may have unwittingly inherited the traits.

The hard sell can be intimidating, overconfident and off-putting. So how do we instead, catch the monkeys softly?

Don't go in guns blazing like you're there to steal the show. That's not your goal anymore – you're there to build a relationship. You're not automatically entitled to a piece of anyone's pie. Hard selling doesn't work in the realm of dating either, so we can all agree it's not an encouraged bond building technique.

I'd go as far as to say - hard selling is dead. Today's generation of clients has evolved beyond that. They want engagement, added value and genuine connections. Therefore, if you still believe pushing deals down the phone in a Wolf of Wall Street tribute is the way to go about business, your time in this sales era will be short lived.

Step one is getting away from these legacy approaches and opening your eyes to a new style of selling. Stop being sleazy in sales, and start being the type of person your clients want to date.

Chapter 2 - Chat up lines

Let's think about your introduction to your clients as a chat up line. Your company has probably been kind enough to provide a standard template they'd like you to use. I bet you have it memorised, and can deliver it in the first 10 seconds of the call before your target even has a chance to speak. I'm also sure 90% of these calls go the same way. It's not surprising really - when you use the same opening, you'll get the same response.

Let's have a look at dating. Would you use the same chat up line on every person you wanted to pursue? Worse yet, would you send it out on a mass email? With a mail merge for the names?

To clients it's pretty obvious when they're in receipt of a copy and paste job, or are being recited a generic opener. Usually they will write it off as spam and promptly delete or shut down your call. Busy clients are not going to take the time to respond when you haven't taken the time to present something thoughtful. Standardisation is an effective way of demonstrating you don't deem your clients worthy of the effort it takes to make the approach personal and relevant.

A good chat up line is one that conveys you've done your homework, or at least got lucky with your subject of choice. If you want to make it past the first phase of the call or meeting, you need a 'hook.' Something that strikes a chord with your client and begins to warm them up. Let's do better than making bland observations about the weather or forced admiration of their offices. A strong chat up line gets you off on the right foot. A weak one can close your window of opportunity instantly.

Anyone responsible for the buying decisions of a company will undoubtedly be bombarded by sales calls. Most of these pitches sound the same – staged, scripted and poorly prepared. Those of you who have had the pleasure of online dating, may have experienced similar strategies from vying suitors, sliding into your direct messages with universal chat up lines. Even on LinkedIn we've become victims of unattractive pleas for attention. The downfall of these approaches is that they are unlikely to inspire enthusiasm. They may not even inspire a response.

These days, we have so much information at our fingertips. It's strange that we rarely use this to personalise our sales interactions, to at least prove we have thought about their business and have decided they're worth the chase. We want our clients to feel sought after - ideally flattered - that they're getting some well angled attention. Online profiles, company websites and social media are littered with breadcrumbs of personal facts that we can leverage to create effective chat up lines. People divulge these titbits because we instinctively want people to know us better.

I'll give you an example. On my LinkedIn profile, you can quickly derive:

- I've not been in my job for long
- I care about animals
- I went to Strathclyde Business School
- There are also a few hints that I might be sporty

14

How could this translate into a practical sales/dating pitch? Include any of the following:

- "How are you enjoying the new job?"
- "I see you like animals, do you have pets?"
- "I know (mutual contact) that went to the same university as you. They said it was a great place to study. How did you find it?"
- "Are you following Wimbledon this year?"

The inclusion of personalised questions makes clients immediately more likely to give you the time of day. Why? Because it demonstrates you've used initiative and care to get to know them before you've picked up the phone or wandered into the meeting. You've managed to open with a subject that's relevant to them. They're assured it's not the duplicated spam you've hit up all your other prospects with that same day. And your communication will stand out against the drivel they're used to receiving.

A common reason we don't do this already is laziness. Spending an extra 5-10 minutes compiling research and creating something unique for each client may not fit in nicely with your busy schedule. Some days it's hard enough to tick the boxes and keep your head above water. At least sending emails en masse feels like getting a lot of work done, and probably looks good on the figures. I'm a huge fan of economies of effort, so I take your point caller, and here's why it's still the lazier option:

10 calls or emails a day, all using the same template = response rate 10% (if you're lucky)

5 calls or emails a day, using bespoke, well thought through communication = response rate 30%

More responses = higher chance of relationship = higher chance of business = higher chance of ££££

So what else can we learn from dating? Compliments* tend to be a popular preamble in traditional dating, however these don't transpose so well into sales. The reason is because complimenting people you don't know that well (clients) can be dicey. If a stranger in the street unexpectedly tells me I'm good looking, I'll either be naively besotted or I'll smile worriedly and walk faster. The latter is more likely. Complimenting your prospects is similar in that it can sound fake, desperate, or worse case, creepy. A tactic that can work well though, is being the person who delivers a compliment that originated from another source. We call this 'sharing the messenger.'

In real life

A colleague of mine received an email saying...

"I'm writing to introduce myself as we both know Person X and they said you were brilliant to work with and cared a lot about getting the right procurement partners for your company."

See what happened there? The compliment came from someone else but this salesperson was kind enough to deliver it. Prospective Client X is instantly chuffed something nice was said about them and it softens them up to the seller. It doesn't come across as inappropriate as there's reference to a common point of contact. Client

X is more likely to respond to a kind message, and also not be rude - in case it gets back to the mutual friend.

The obvious pitfall is that you need a shared connection to say something flattering about your target client. The easy way to get this is to ABN – "always be networking." LinkedIn makes this simple as you can see who knows who straightaway. You can approach the mutual connection and ask for a quick overview of your target to see if there's a commendation you can use.

Another angle you can try, is if you are dealing with one person at a company, and want to pursue an employee in another area, use your existing contact for the ploy. It's as simple as, "Do you know such and such? What are they like?" As soon as a positive trait is mentioned, write it down and use it as your co-created compliment.

Surely you would just ask Employee 1 to recommend you to Employee 2 instead? You can do, but in my experience, people generally don't like being told what to do because someone else said so. If anything, it can make them more reluctant to use you because it takes away their chance to judge you for themselves. This might not always be the case depending on the client, but often this is how it can feel. Humans like choice. Decision makers like control and the ability to choose suppliers. It's their job, and it makes them feel empowered. So, don't take this power away from them. Use sharing the messenger, or a tailored chat up line instead for better results.

*If you ever feel the genuine need to pay someone a compliment, do so. Spontaneous compliments are good things if they are sincere. Just don't use them to fill a silence or to get on your client's good side. Fake compliments are easy to spot, and it can lower their impression of you, so don't bother.

Chapter 3 - It's the little things

In dating, we do little things to show our partners we care. Whether it's picking them up a Magnum for dessert or folding their laundry, small acts can add tremendous value to a relationship. Find a way to do these for your clients, and you'll see the impact in this relationship too.

In real life

A few years ago, one of my best clients liked coffee. I'm sure most of my clients liked coffee so we'll say this one really loved it. To be specific, she was partial to a:

"Venti, skimmed milk, triple shot, caramel latte with whipped cream."

Not the simplest or most logical order, however every time we went out to visit we brought her one. And she cherished it. We were the only salespeople to even ask how she liked her coffee, never mind commit it to memory, endure the judgemental looks from Starbucks staff, and deliver it hot to her office. It cost a whole £4 but the return was thousands of pounds in business and a hearty relationship. We were invited out a lot.

Why did a coffee have the power to fortify the business? Because little things can make a huge difference to how you are perceived. They can actually carry more weight than something grand and flashy, which let's be honest, we rarely have the budget to do anyway. If you're able to remember something as personal as the above coffee order, and present it as a small gesture of kindness, it will make your prospect feel special. Like they're valued. Like they're not "just another client." And don't get me wrong, the sales side of things with this client was far from a breeze; we had challenges aplenty. But that coffee gave us a lot more breathing space than another supplier without the caffeine would have had.

In real life, again

I've experienced the touching impact small gestures can have first-hand. In my client shoes, I had a meeting with a new supplier booked. It was an average meeting, he was a pleasant chap, and the service discussed seemed to meet our needs. But then, five other salespeople could probably have offered the same deal. During the meeting, I'd made an offhand comment about my perpetual lack of pens. The meeting adjourned and I spent the rest of my week being pitched to by their competitors. However, come Monday morning, a mystery package arrived on my desk. It was plastered in stamps and had been hand written in a scrawl I didn't recognise. I was pleasantly surprised to find it contained 10 new, branded pens and a quick note hoping I would no longer be without. They got the business.

Why? If a salesperson can pick up on an offhand comment and proactively go out their way to send a solution to a problem that was barely hinted at - well just think how they'll perform with a real piece of work. This small act made them stand out amongst their rivals and had me liking them, impressed by them and looking forward to working with them. It was a taster of a) how they treat their customers i.e. meeting every need, and b) how they go about business i.e. taking the initiative to add value.

The key to these small acts is they shouldn't be an implied trade. Yes, in both the above examples the parties were of course hoping to gain business, but it wasn't a case of "Well if you give me your money I'll bring you out coffee and pens." It doesn't have the same warming feel to it when it's leveraged as an exchange. The recipe for perfectly executing these gestures is that they should be done without expectations, and before you have any reason to do so. It's not a case of keeping your client sweet or offering gifts to make up for something gone wrong. It's about demonstrating from an early stage that you're actively listening, and are happy to complement the commerce with small acts of kindness.

This is easily one of the most effective techniques I've ever witnessed. Some of us do these acts instinctively while others have a target and an assigned budget for entertaining clients. Try and go beyond the cliché lunches or after work drinks. While this is good fun, and certainly softens the professional dynamic, it tends to be a strategy used for clients you're already established with. It rarely helps in the case of winning new business. After all, who is going to voluntarily sacrifice their personal time to have a cocktail with a group of people they don't know and don't need? It's the working equivalent of a blind date.*

Final in real life

I used to work with a guy who was master of the little things. He sent 'Get Well Soon' cards, 'Congrats on the new job' flowers, and once he dropped off a bottle of champagne for a receptionist's engagement (this works on gatekeepers too). He basically treated his clients the

21

same way he would treat a girlfriend when it came to sending tokens of affection. He only had about 6 clients but they used him exclusively for years and would never dream of going anywhere else with their business. His little things were the reason why.

So, the secret to wild sales success is actually coffee, cards and pens. Who knew? These actions aren't ostentatious or overwhelming. You don't have to throw rose petals at someone's feet to impress them. Interweave small acts of kindness with client relationships along with your personal ones, and watch them start to flourish in a whole new way.

*My definition of a blind date is spending time with a stranger in a social context where politeness prevents you from escaping.

Chapter 4 - 'Saw this, and thought of you'

Reliance on technology isn't ideal when it comes to romantic relationships - however in sales, there could be an exception. In the right circumstances, technology can be used to enhance the long-distance relationships you have with your clients. After all, you don't see your clients every day (perhaps not at all) and you definitely don't have the option of making them dinner or giving them a massage at night.

In this digital age, it would be crazy not to take advantage of the tools we have at our disposal to supplement how we interact with clients. The suppliers I've had the strongest relationships with have an interaction split of 50% talking about core business and 50% talking about anything else. If you are the type of salesperson who only ever speaks about BAU, you will struggle to build real rapport and consequently, a connection that transcends the transactional process.

There are several ways to make up that other 50%. In your chat up lines, you will converse about relevant opening topics, and in upcoming chapters DMCs and War of the Robots, you'll broaden the horizons even more. But for now, we'll look at how we can use technology to intertwine additional themes and frequency of touch points.

In real life

In a new job, I found myself responsible for IT recruitment of the company. This wasn't something I'd done before so the learning curve was steep to say the least. I had engaged with some suppliers to outsource what we needed to until I found my feet. One day I got a call from reception advising someone had visited and left something for me. I popped down to find a copy of the latest industry guide for the IT job market. A salesperson had dropped it off with a handwritten post-it saying she hoped it'd help give me some insight. She hadn't bothered to hassle me for a meeting; she hadn't even asked if it was something I wanted. It was very much a case of, she had access to information that might be useful and she popped it on my lap.

"Saw this – thought of you" is an effective way of letting your clients know that you're thinking of them, you care about alerting them to material that is helpful, or you've simply found something to put a smile on their face. This could be in the form of news articles, industry statistics, a relevant blog, competitors' movements or even a meme to make them laugh. We tag our partners and friends in stuff all the time, so why should it be any different when it comes to our clients? Information flies past us on a daily basis, so pick out what's relevant and feed it to the people who will appreciate it.

Date night

About 8 years ago one of my pals was living the coffee shop barista dream. He had been dating a girl but things had fizzled out due to university schedules and general busyness. After several week's lapse in contact, he received a link to a news article about a coffee shop employee who had robbed the company and jetted off to the Bahamas. She'd added text asking, "Is this where you've been?" It rekindled their communication.

It can be hard to maintain a client relationship when you only have reason to contact them sporadically. Phoning "just for a chat" can be annoying and pointless, unless they really love the sound of your voice. Unfortunately, clients often have better things to do, such as their day job. Small touches of low key communication can keep you in their minds without an overkill of superfluous calls, emails and meetings.

Another facet of traditional sales culture that's sorely misaligned with modern day clients is the KPI constraints on communication. Common sense tells us that in sales, we will have to take active steps towards winning new business. A higher dose of common sense tells us we will probably have to speak to people more than once to do so. However, the illogical way sales managers have quantified and confined this in numbers and accepted forms is mind boggling. Who came up with the theory that a ridiculously high number of cold calls per week works? Is it a spray and pray mentality? Did this guarantee world domination 30 years ago? Well we're 30 years on now and KPIs need to change, adapt and evolve, to better align with next generation clients and the advancements of technology.

In real life

In a previous sales job, I had to call 50 clients a week, and ensure I continued to call them at least every 4 weeks in frequency. Anyone who's decent at maths will understand the impracticable cumulative effect this sum has. And we wonder why it feels like there's not enough hours in the day? Even if we had nothing new to talk about (and I was very aware I was being a pest), we were instructed to pick up the phone anyway.

These days we chat to clients on LinkedIn, and usually email them more than we speak to them - both of which are practical and less overwhelming for the clients. But sometimes there's no incentive to do this other than good judgment. Our KPIs often dictate the opposite. In our busy commercial worlds, the chances of missing a call are high, whereas taking time to get back to emails or catch up on LinkedIn messages is a normal part of the day. As long as sales directors continue to push for quantity over quality and ignore the other forms of contact available, they will struggle to engage with today's clients.

The next generation of clients has grown up regarding texts, emails, IMs and DMs to be legitimate forms of communication. They're used to being able to order a pizza, book a hotel or plan a holiday without having to speak to anyone, so they have an all-time low tolerance for unnecessary exchanges.

Make each interaction you have with your clients count. Make the contact worthwhile for both sides. Have enjoyable conservations, send personalised emails, share content that's relevant and timely. Add value through the inclusion of current channels and get away from the unnatural touch points if you can. You don't start dating someone and think, "Right, I better call them once every day and arrange 3 dates per week including 1 sleepover." You interact with them when it feels right and is suitable for both parties. Next time you go to pick up the phone or arrange a meeting, consciously decide if you are doing it because it deepens the relationship or because it ticks a box on your KPIs.

Chapter 5 - Ghosting

Hopefully you've been fortunate enough to make it this far in life without being ghosted. For those of you who are unfamiliar with the term, ghosting is:

'The act of suddenly ceasing all communication with someone the subject is dating, but no longer wishes to date. This is done in hopes that the ghostee will just "get the hint" and leave the subject alone, as opposed to the subject simply telling them he/she is no longer interested.'

Urban Dictionary, 2017

This technique is commonplace on the contemporary dating scene. These days, it's just too easy to ignore an IM or block someone, rather than compose a heartfelt explanatory text.

As we continue on the theme of being nice humans to deal with, it should come as no surprise we're recommending not ghosting people in sales or in your love life. In fact, in sales you should strive to go to the opposite extreme and **always be available to your clients**. A terrifying concept for some of you, I'm sure. However, there is nothing more encouraging than when you start seeing someone new and they possess the ability to text back in a timely manner, or answer the phone when you call. It shows they're interested and keen for things to progress. And this is how your clients should feel too.

We are all about push communications when on the hunt for new business. We are the ones calling and requesting to see them in the initial stages. Our hearts skip a beat when we receive a call back or a satisfying email reply to our advances. But strangely, as the relationship becomes less novel and more part of the daily grind, we have a tendency to go to ground.

A client might become particularly taxing or there may be challenges with the service. You may no longer want to answer and talk about issues or listen to complaints. It can wear you down, and you inadvertently begin to ghost them.

The phone calls go unreturned and the emails sit in our inbox for days. The logic is to buy ourselves enough time to find a solution (or get a bit of headspace), and in the interim, dodge their attempts to get in touch. We'll cunningly have our colleagues tell them we're "just on another call" or "I can't see him at his desk right now." We'll keep moving their name further down our to do list until we're in the right frame of mind to deal with it.

However lack of response to your clients' attempts to speak are the dating equivalent of leaving a text on read receipt (✓✓) - and no one enjoys that.

In real life

I've worked in offices where it was common practice to shun calls from clients until you knew what they were about. The rationale was that you would only speak to them when you had prepared an answer. So, in practice Client X would call, another member of the team would intercept it and find out what the issue was. They'd then pass this info on to the salesperson who was meant to be dealing with it. Client X would leave the message and not hear anything for a few hours (or days) until their consultant eventually responded with a solution up their sleeve.

I get the reasoning. Rather than risk being caught on the hop, you can buy some time, find the information or resolution, and appear totally unflustered when you resume communication. However, for every time you don't answer that call or reply to that email, you chip away at your client's perception of you.

From a client POV, being unable to get a hold of someone who was, only a few weeks ago, speaking to you at every possible opportunity, can send mixed signals. It might make them feel that now their business is yours, you're not going to make as much effort as you did at the start. You're complacent. You take them for granted. They are no longer your number one priority. The same way it would feel if this happened in a romantic setting.

When you're dating someone, and they go AWOL for a few hours or days, what do you assume? You assume the worst. Something bad has happened (we are a cynical lot after all). You might think they're no longer that bothered about you. You'd feel disheartened, let down and probably a touch rejected.

The same can be said of your clients when they're left wondering why you haven't got back to them. They may speculate there's an issue with the service, a delivery or a deadline you said you were going to meet. And the longer they're left to think like this, the more they're losing faith in you and questioning the merits of the relationship you have built so far.

There may be absolutely nothing wrong at all. You may just be having a chaotic day. But a quick email to explain and that you'll call later, will put their minds at ease.

You know those times you phone your mum and it rings out and you mentally note how useless she would be in an actual emergency? Your clients get that same feeling when they're calling you and it keeps going to voicemail.

Things don't always go smoothly. No one has a job where things go to plan all the time. However, when you work in sales, sometimes it can feel that things go wrong more often than they go right.

No matter which side of the equation you're on – client or salesperson - you'll usually have more respect for the other party if they are upfront and transparent when plans are going pear-shaped. Think about your boss, your colleagues, even your family and friends. Are there people in these circles who prefer to tackle issues head on, or stick their head in the sand? If you've ever bought a house and had your lawyer or estate agent go MIA during the process, you'll know how troubling it is. The point is that people generally prefer to be kept in the loop during difficult times, rather than receive an unpleasant surprise later. These are the times when remaining open and communicative count most. And these are exactly the times not to ghost people.

In real life

I'd arranged with a salesperson to have x number of products by a specific date. A few days from the deadline I received a call from her to explain that several things had fallen through at their end, and unfortunately, they weren't going to be able to fulfil it on time. She described what had happened and asked for an extension. Rather than being miffed and finding someone else to supply, I agreed to the extra time. Why? Because she was honest. She didn't leave it until the last minute to tell me. I had plenty of warning and was kept up to date. Most importantly, she didn't bloody ghost me. She just said it how it was and I valued that. The majority of clients are reasonable enough to accept business doesn't go perfectly all the time, and if they like you, these occasions will be regarded as very minor bumps in the road.

Set yourself an SLA for your clients. Force yourself to always answer when you can. Ensure anything you miss is replied to within an hour of picking it up. Let your clients know when you're going to be out of the office and when you're coming back.

Your ability to be available and responsive directly links to how reliable you're perceived to be. If there are two salespeople to choose from: one who is good at what they do but you can never get a hold of them, or one who occasionally drops the ball, but you're kept fully in the loop and can talk through any issues as and when they arise – you'll always pick the second supplier to work with. If you don't believe me, ask your clients what they'd prefer and see how they answer.

Your client is your partner. Don't leave them hanging in the dark.

Chapter 6 - Gratitude

Everyone loves to feel appreciated. Yet sometimes we forget to say the words out loud because of the labels we give people. Our partner is our other half so surely, they know we love them and are grateful for them. Our employees are paid to do their job, so we don't need to say thanks for fulfilling that. Our colleagues are on the same team as us, so of course they should be helping out where possible. And our clients are our income, so it goes without saying we appreciate their work, time, patience, opportunity and collaboration, doesn't it?

Wrong. In many case we assume (and we know in sales assuming is bad) that our clients know we value their business. And it certainly doesn't hurt to say it more often.

In real life

As a client, I'd had a meeting with some salespeople to hammer out a few issues. Discussions went back and forth until we eventually agreed an action plan that everyone was happy with. We decided to move forwards and recover the situation, rather than a termination of service which was also on the cards. It can't have been a pleasant meeting for them, being on the receiving end of a thinly veiled commercial ultimatum. However, they ended the meeting by saying they were grateful – that it'd been brought to their attention, that they'd been out to discuss, and that we'd continue working together. Often these meetings are ended on apologies but gratitude's an effective way to go.

Being vocal about gratitude with your client's business, and anyone else who helps you on the way (colleagues, gatekeepers, even your boss) will begin to embed this into your sales mindset. As the gratitude becomes inbuilt, you'll naturally begin to treat the people involved with extra care. You'll be more patient, open to different points of view, and eager to deepen the connection because you're continually acknowledging what it means to you. You may even stimulate some thankfulness in return, after all, how frequently do your clients declare they "truly value your services"?

I used to say, "Thank you, I appreciate it" twenty times a day to various parties to ensure I got the message across. It's a simple thing to express, but can have tremendous impact, especially if your competitors aren't making it so crystal clear. If you appear grateful for something, people are less likely to whip it away from you when there's a setback. They will know what the partnership means to you. They'll be more likely to give you the opportunity to rectify any issues, rather than move swiftly on to another option, without giving you a second thought. After all, it would be a little heartless to do so after you'd chatted them up, memorised their coffee order, always been one call away and were now expressing sincere gratitude for having them in your life (or on your forecast).

Just as we don't want to ghost our clients, we want to make sure our clients don't feel it's ok to ghost us. Stating the value of the relationship is another way of safeguarding against presumptions they don't mean much to you, and that losing their business wouldn't be a big deal.

The other thing that's worth mentioning from the above sales story, is that the salespeople we met were weirdly enthusiastic. As we know, in sales...

"service meetings" can translate to

"a drilling, followed by an uphill struggle to retain the business."

Because of this, we often face them with dread. We think about possible rebuttals on the journey there; we mentally note our negotiation boundaries before we come face to face. We may even start the meeting more reserved than usual, holding our breath to find out how bad the damage is.

But these guys just bounded right in, smiling brightly, and eager to hear all about the critical failings. Why? Remember when you were taught that objections are secretly buying signals? Well these salespeople knew that complaints are indicators that your client is still interested. They're still invested enough to want to discuss it, and that discussion can be easily transformed into the opportunity to recover/improve.

When relationships don't mean much, the risk of being ghosted is higher, and clients are extremely guilty of doing this to us. You know when you haven't received a reply to your third consecutive email and reception no longer puts through your calls? That's you being ghosted by your client. You didn't mean enough to them to get the explanatory text. However, if you're invited out for a service meeting, the good news is they're not done with you yet.

So along with being grateful, it's handy to make a conscious effort to be a positive force in the venture, like the salespeople at the service meeting. Every office is bestowed at least one colleague who swirls around in a cloud of negative commentary, and it's worth checking this isn't you. If a client presents you with constructive feedback, it means they're giving you the insight you need to address what's not working for them. Even in real relationships, we don't always get this chance, so it's incredibly lucky to get it in sales.

Be positive when this happens. Our jobs are challenging and indisputably come with adrenaline fuelled highs and kick in the teeth lows. When you've had the week from hell and you're in front of a client being told that your offering is below par, it can be hard not to close your eyes and groan. But make it your aim to meet these situations with an optimistic outlook. Take it in your stride and get into recovery mode. Present solutions, not self-pity. Be accountable and action orientated, rather than mopey and despondent. A little shared empathy with clients in times of trouble can be a good response, just make sure this isn't all you do, or worse, don't bring them down with you.

Keep your winning, auspicious game face on and when you turn things around, as you inevitably will, make sure you say you're grateful.

Chapter 7 - Trust me, I'm good

It's no secret that in relationships trust issues are a big thing. Trusting your partner can give you a happy carefree run, while mistrust can tarnish every part of it. When it boils down to it, trust can be the deciding factor in what makes a relationship a success or a failure.

Often, when we meet someone new, it becomes apparent that the experience of a previous romance has left doubt on their mind and distrust in their mouth. Maybe they were let down, lied to or given false hope. Either way they are likely to carry this with them, and instinctively regard you through suspicious, beady eyes.

For clients, there can be an undercurrent of scepticism when courting new salespeople. Rightly so, they would be silly to trust you from the outset when you haven't proved if you're "one of the good guys" yet. If they're a decision maker in a company, they will probably have had their fair share of disappointments and broken promises, and this can create a jaded attitude towards everyone in our line of work. It's almost like when they first start dealing with you, they take your word with a pinch of salt and are secretly waiting for you to screw it up. The perception of salespeople being devious in general doesn't help our case, especially when trying to win new business.

But it's easier to build trust than you think. There's one simple rule of thumb for this and it's that **actions speak louder than words**. And don't worry, there're no grand gestures involved in this technique either. You won't be

.ıg trust falls, leaps of faith or that amazing lift from
ırty Dancing with your clients (sadly).

Trust starts off small, with baby steps. You need to
construct it brick by brick. And you do this by following
through on what you say. Every. Single. Time. Making sure
your actions back up your words for the most trivial of
deeds from the very start of the relationship. For
example, saying you'll call at 2pm and then you call at
2pm. Promising to send a follow up email and then
actually sending the follow up email (not darting off to
make coffee number 7 instead).

These may seem like insignificant events, and to some
customers they may not matter at all. But if you're
committed to proving yourself to a client, standing out
against your competitors, and untangling yourself from
the fickle sales stereotype, you'll have to execute your
actions to a tee.

Let's look at it in dating. You've started seeing someone
new. They said they'll give you a call at 8pm. You wait by
the phone, it rings at 8.30pm. Cool, only half an hour late
and it's early days. You've arranged drinks on Friday, they
cancel on the Thursday as can't make it any more. No
worries, these things happen. You're out for lunch. They
said they'd bring that top you left at theirs. They forgot.
Does this person ever do what they say?

Now imagine you weren't even bothered about dating
this person anyway, and you have 50 other admirers
swearing they can do better. Do you wait on your current
suitor getting their act together, or do you just turn to

someone else? These are the choices your clients are faced with every day.

Set yourself missions. Every time you have an interaction with your client, make a promise with a time or deadline attached, and push yourself to fulfil it. Fulfil it a little early to really blow their mind. Turn up to the meeting on time. Bring out the information you said you would. Actively go out your way to make commitments, set timescales, and then complete them meticulously. Do this constantly and consistently, and watch as your client's scepticism melts away and they begin to regard you as a man/woman of your word. They start to feel like they're in safe hands. They eventually believe they've found a salesperson who *actually does what they say they're going to*. And as a client, that's the ultimate dream.

We all have competitors, and there are only minor things that set us apart. Our prices or products or service offering may have slight variations, but ultimately, **you** are the core differentiator. The difference maker. In sales, it's the smallest factors that have the biggest impact on if a client regards you as good to work with. Can they get a hold of you? Do they like speaking to you? Can you stick to your word? Whether they spell it out or not, these trivialities are what will win you clients, protect your accounts, and have you branded as great to deal with when they discuss you with their peers.

By laying a foundation of trust in the initial stages and reinforcing it repeatedly, you'll compound the interest until you get to the point where your client simply takes you at your word. Because all evidence that they've witnessed up until this point confirms you fulfil commitments. They will literally have no reason to feel that you're ever going to lie or let them down. Then when you go in for the big sale, the crucial tender, or the pitch for the largest piece of the pie, your client has no reason to doubt that you'll be able to deliver what you say you will. Because that's all you've ever done. The trust, and business, is yours.

In all forms of relationships, actions speak louder than words.

The other time trust comes in handy, is when a client needs to feel comfortable bringing up certain topics. This could be when things aren't working, when they'd like to voice a complaint, or perhaps just to present some constructive feedback. Sometimes asking for changes in service such as less contact or more attention can be awkward to ask for.

If you've been in a management position, you'll know you have some staff you trust to take feedback well, and other staff you know are likely to argue enthusiastically with every point you make. Sadly, as a manager, you're paid to deal with both these scenarios and there's no getting away from that. But for clients, it's easy to avoid working with salespeople who don't digest negative comments well. Therefore, you need to make it clear you're not one of them.

People in trusting relationships are able to speak about sensitive matters because they trust their spouse will be open to hearing it. They have faith it won't be dismissed or taken as a personal attack. If you've ever had a partner who didn't take disagreements well, you may be familiar with the feeling that some conversations are "just not worth the hassle." This is not how we want our clients to feel. Luckily, we can develop trust to guarantee our clients are confident that no subject is off limits, even if it's not going to be pleasant. Without this assurance, they may just not bother at all, and you'll be left wondering why their account has suddenly diminished.

In real life

There have been a few times I've had to give feedback as a client, and there's nothing worse than working with salespeople who don't take it well. Reactions have ranged from blank expressions to stunned disbelief to outright insistence that they weren't to blame. These reactions aren't productive, as they render the feedback void and the client is left in the same unsatisfactory situation as when they brought it up. When a supplier refutes feedback, there's no way of moving the relationship forward, and the only option may be to move away and find someone else to work with.

As with all trust issues, if you have experienced them once, you'll be wary of it again. If your client has been in this predicament before, they may not trust that you're keen for feedback and consequently won't tell you when things could be improved. When the service is no longer working to their satisfaction, they will avoid shedding light on it and inconspicuously move on to another supplier. This tends to happen a lot in sales and goes hand in hand with being ghosted. Sadly, so many of us lose business without knowing it because we weren't doing something we didn't know our clients wanted - it hardly seems fair.

So how can you ensure your clients trust you to have these conversations? How can you guarantee you're given every opportunity to enhance your service and avoid unwittingly losing them to your competitors?

Invite them to give feedback. Invite it frequently and encouragingly. Some people simply don't enjoy or can't be bothered raising issues, and will refrain from doing so unless actively prompted. So you need to ask for it. Do this at the end of every call or arrange regular meetings specifically to check on contentment levels. Send out quarterly online surveys if you need to. This doesn't have to be a negative addition. It's a helpful and trust building exercise for both you and your clients.

In real life

I took a punt and asked a new supplier to attend a conference call to be briefed on upcoming work. There were several managers on the call, and this sales chap was included by my invitation. We all joined the meeting... except for him. I killed five minutes with introductions and pleasantries hoping he was running late. Nine minutes into the call and still no sign of him. I stuck everyone on mute and called his office. He eventually appeared and we made the most of the time we had left for the briefing. Afterwards I voiced my concern about his lateness. I suspected he'd completely forgotten he was meant to be on the call. Not a great start, and I was worried the work from him was going to be haphazard. He gave a sincere apology and promised we'd never receive substandard service again. Now every single time we speak, he asks if there's anything he can do better. "Any tweaks to service or any areas for improvement?" The fact he makes a point of asking sticks in my mind, and I know if there's ever anything that needs to be said, he'll be happy to hear it. He's become one of our go to suppliers.

You know when you speak to anyone in customer service, and at the end you get the staple "Is there anything else I can help you with today?" – that's all this technique is about. It's the same as building up the perception that you keep your word. By incorporating positive behaviours such as seeking out suggestions, your clients will begin to see this as an integral part of the relationship.

Challenge yourself to regularly ask for feedback and keep the lines of communication gaping open. I used to finish my calls with "Any questions or concerns?" Still do. These questions take less than 10 seconds to ask yet will verify you're not flying blind in any of your relationships. Deploy your trust building techniques successfully and you'll clients will simultaneously put stock in your word, and be certain that they can address any challenges with you on side.

Chapter 8 - DMCs

We're going to level up here and move from chat up lines to DMCs. I got this acronym from Love Island and have surmised it stands for Deep Meaningful Conversations. Feel free to let me know otherwise and I'll revoke this whole chapter.

So DMCs - You know the conversations where you go off on a tangent and wind up discussing how loud the big bang was or if plants have feelings? Well these might seem like a waste of time, but if you're lucky enough to encounter these with your clients, go with it.

I don't know the science behind it but DMCs have some sort of magical ability to transform relationships. There is nothing more unifying than having an intimate discussion with someone about an abstract concept. Think about all the times you were out in the smoking area talking to strangers, or in the kitchen at a house party, or in bed with a new acquaintance at 1am, and you got onto a random subject that had you talking all night. These are the types of conversations that happen when people are getting closer. You've reached a point where you're relaxed enough to speak uninhibitedly and ponder the world with another soul. But how do these help with sales?

In real life

There's a supplier who consistently goes out his way to avoid talking about business. At first, I thought it was strange he was more concerned about the fact I was an only child than where his next piece of work was coming from, however I soon realised that this was a valuable relationship building technique. By always directing the conversation towards non-work-related issues, we ended up having what can only be described as great conversations. We've psychoanalysed our childhoods, discussed favourite boxsets; even shared financial plans and future career options. He tells me about the new moped he's buying to drive down to the beach, and I tell him about my flatmate who drinks like a fish. An outsider listening in would guess we're not being very productive, however these unconventional interactions have added a new level of engagement to our work. I could shoot the breeze with this guy all day. I enjoy speaking to him. I'll never not answer his calls or reply to his emails because it'd be like ignoring a friend.

I've noticed that the best client/salesperson relationships have a subject matter split of 50% work and 50% play. The reason non-business-related conversations work so well is because they soften up the professional facade. The more time you spend talking to your clients as you would your friends, the less of a 'salesperson' you become, and the more they start to see you as just a 'person'. People buy from people, people talk to people, people date people. And that's how you want your clients to see you.

Now you don't have to quiz your clients on their fondest childhood memory or demand philosophical answers to get these conversations going. People naturally bring up what they want to talk about – we're a little self-centred that way. You just have to keep your ears open and pick up on it. Someone might mention their kids, a football team, their plans for the weekend. Ask a follow up question. If they speak freely you can take this as confirmation they're happy to share in more detail. Basic topics lead onto more interesting ones if you let them. That's the beauty of DMCs - it's usually something basic that starts them, and by the end, you're left wondering how you got on to what really happened at the end of the Sopranos and if the robots will win the war to come.

It should be noted that in order to get clients to relax their tongues, you may have to share something to begin with. Most people don't go out on a limb and start describing their family tree unless someone has prompted them to do so by showing their cards first. Whether it's what you did with your weekend, what your plans are for Christmas or who you wanted to win Love Island, give your viewpoint and invite them to match it with theirs.

Whether we admit it or not, we often have difficulty getting hold of clients because they don't actually want to speak to us. They associate it with hard work. They see your number flash up and assume it's another sales pitch, a negotiation or an issue they'll have to deal with, and automatically recoil. If these are the only topics you ever talk about, then of course they'll assume that's why you're getting in touch. However, if you're able to balance getting business done, with enjoyable interaction, your clients will find it less taxing to hear from you. They may even come to find your dealings quite pleasant if they get a tête-à-tête out of it too.

Date night

How well I remember a date depends on which of these three categories it falls into:

1. *I remember it because it was great*
2. *I remember it because it was so bad*
3. *I barely remember it at all because I guess it was unremarkable*

The reason for which dates go into what category is as follows:

1. *Great conversation, brought something different to the table, didn't act assumptively*
2. *Terrible one-sided conversation, bad angles, tried to score a quick win, told my friends about it afterwards*
3. *Must have been so bland or generic that I switched off*

This is exactly the same way clients will classify your calls. You only ever want to be placed in the first group. The other two options will never result in a home run.

As a client, there are certain salespeople I'll always pick up for because I know I'll get a natter and a few laughs, as well as something practical done. It's like being able to chat to a mate in the middle of your working day. Who wouldn't want to kill twenty minutes doing that? If you can disguise it as business and make your clients not regret answering your calls, brilliant. It's a win-win.

The more you're able to break down the perception that you're just another salesperson chasing money, the likelier it is that you'll get to speak to your clients. Unbarred interaction allows you to develop relationships, and ultimately prosper from them. So next time a client brings up an incidental topic, don't fret about getting off track. Revel in the conversation, turn it into a DMC and heighten the way you engage with your clients.

Chapter 9 - Who gives a fuck?

Now I'm not endorsing swearing in work or on dates, but I am advocating communicating in the way you naturally would. I'm still mildly impressed when someone wanders into a work meeting and announces the project's gone "tits up" and everything's "a fucking disaster." Talking like this is uncensored and authentic. It shows somebody is relaxed and speaking freely, and that's exactly how you want the people you're in business with to be. So, let's stop stifling how we speak to our clients.

In sales, we sometimes put ourselves on the back foot. We know we need our clients more than they need us and as such, we try and change ourselves to appear more desirable. Perhaps we speak a little more formally, use bigger words, and maintain politeness as though our life depends on it. But you need to feel comfortable speaking openly in your sales relationships. You'll never have natural engaging conversations, or honest, heartfelt debates, if you're always proofing what you're going to say before you say it. You need to feel safe telling them when the plans are going to hell or when they're being unreasonable. Ultimately, you need to be your most genuine self if you want to establish real relationships. So, get rid of the filter on your mouth and be prepared to be amazed when you utter the word "fuck" and your clients don't disappear in a puff of smoke. There's a good chance they'll smile coyly and swear back.

I used to do a lot of work with construction companies and it was like selling to Billy Connolly. When you slide into corporate environments or into your first sales job, you may be told to "smarten up, speak properly and don't swear at the clients." This is true, don't swear *at* them (any customer can be frustrating but wait until you put the phone down please).

They say people who swear frequently are more honest and that's the subliminal impression it gives. When someone is swearing away happily you know they're not putting on an act or trying too hard to impress anybody. They are comfortable enough in their own character, that they don't need to mould it fit an audiences' expectations. So, if you're a salesperson sitting in a meeting, and you're truly confident in your abilities, why feel the need to be anything but your authentic self?

In real life

The human tone is engaging. When I first started writing articles, I kept them very formal and straight-laced. I used proper grammar and punctuation, no colloquial phrases, and proof read them a million times. I was hesitant to be too relaxed and personal in case people didn't like that, which would feel like they didn't like me. The articles weren't very colourful or stimulating. They were just safe. Then I got preoccupied moving house, had neglected writing for a few months and thought it'd be good to hammer out an article on a lunch break. I glanced at it twice and hit publish. It was frank, sarcy, a little cynical with a touch of droll, and completely unpolished. Basically, the same tone in which thoughts run through my head. I actually apologised to readers as I thought they'd be offended by the lack of grammatical composure. This raw, off the cuff, 500-word literacy minefield was one of my best received pieces. Why? It sounded like a person speaking rather than a news reporter without sound. It was more like the way I speak than something I'd subjected to a variety of checks to strain any personality out.

So that's how I write now, as within this book. It's more engaging when people are themselves. If you write all your emails and marketing in your true voice, and hold your client meetings and calls to the same standard, you'll be astonished at how well other humans respond. Don't be scared to relax your tone completely with clients. Whether it's dropping f-bombs or chatting the way you would to a friend, this comfort level moves you past the standard business connotations to an alliance with fresh layers of rapport.

Email 1

There's a supplier who will literally send an email saying,

"How's tricks? The weather's s**t. Can't wait til 5 o'clock for a pint."

Not the most mind-blowing sales prose you've ever seen, but funnily enough, I'll always reply to him. Everyone always replies to him. Why? Firstly, because it feels like a person talking and it'd be rude to ignore it. Secondly, it has the tenor of friendship, so is easy and inviting to write back to.

Email 2

Conversely, the following does not tend to get a response:

"Hi Lauren,

My name is James and I'm a Senior Consultant at World Class Sales. I'm writing to introduce myself as I appreciate we haven't spoken before. I've worked in sales for 900 years and I have a product that is just right for you. It has really convoluted USPs but they sound catchy (we use alliteration) and as luck would have it, we happen to have a promotion running right now for new clients like you. What are the chances!

I'd love the opportunity to take you on this journey and truly explore everything I can offer you and your company. I'll demonstrate what incredible value our generic product has. It will probably save your company millions. I'm a Senior Consultant, after all, so I should know!

When's good for me to call and discuss further?

Kind regards,

James
Senior Consultant"

Ok so that email possesses more personality than usual, but you get the gist of it. Does anything about that email turn you on, and make you want to book in a call with James? No. So why are you sending material like that to your prospective clients? Seriously imagine receiving ten of them a day. And you wonder why customers don't respond. These are sales speeches and people aren't expected to respond to a speech. Speeches are a one-way thing, about a particular topic, from one person's point of view. In my experience, people barely listen to speeches unless they're forced to (like at the annual company conference) so when you present the equivalent on email, you can't blame your clients for hitting delete.

Date night

I went on a first date with a guy who talked about himself a lot. He was a professional poker player – cool job - so at first, I was keen to hear more. Little did I know I was about to endure a six-hour soliloquy. Rather than telling me a bit about him, and then asking about me (you know, a conversation?) we stayed firmly focused on him. He told me about his job, how much he made, the places he'd travelled to and the way the hotels put them up; an overview of the freebies they got at the tournaments and the pros and cons of getting a sponsor. Once he ran out of things to say about his job, he started covering off other subjects including past and present business ventures, investments and his inkling for a new car. Fast forward hours later, I was fake smiling through a stress headache and knocking back the vodkas, while he set a new record for longest time nursing a pint. Finally, he seemed to sense I wasn't going to be booking in for a second date, and scrambled for his ultimate interesting fact – he used to hang out with the guys from Blue (the 00s band). That signalled goodnight from me and a "no need to walk me home."

Back to James' email. Look at how many times it contains the pronoun, I. The pitch was all about him. The date was all about him. Complete focus on oneself and not the other person doesn't work successfully in either example.

In sales, there is so much focus placed on us as individuals, it's no wonder we end up sounding like this by accident. It's our own targets, our own bonus, our own clients. There is heavy emphasis on individual ownership embedded throughout our work. After all there's no 'i' in team, but there are two in 'commission.' So, we tend to think and subsequently talk about ourselves a lot. We speak for hours every day about our company, products and services, our USPs, promotions, our experience - even our job titles get the limelight. Yet all the while, our clients (or dates) are mentally tuning out.

The point is that there is nothing authentic, engaging, honest or human when you talk to your clients in an artificial sales voice. We'll do more on sounding like a human shortly, but in the meantime, compare the two emails and work out why you insist on sending the latter version.

Tell your clients the weather's shit and you hope they're all scanting for a 5pm pint too. If this is how you would naturally talk, see if it works for you. Other than your boss telling you to stop swearing (and they won't care that much if it's working) - you don't have anything to lose by being a bit more yourself. Loosen your tongue and tie, and see what happens. Look how well it worked out for Gordon Ramsay. These clients aren't using you anyway, so who gives a fuck?

Chapter 10 - Make them laugh

We're not all blessed with the natural ability to be quick-witted comedians but we can at least try. Who doesn't enjoy speaking to someone they can joke with? Clients certainly do. You can guarantee if you're a supplier who makes them giggle, you'll get more calls answered, be invited for frequent service visits and receive the coveted ☺ at the end of emails.

Let's be honest, in the world of dating, humour tends to be an essential. If you're spending time with someone as dull as dishwater, it's going to be a long date. Similarly, for clients, it can be a long three-year contract if there aren't any laughs.

Think about it. Your client is in and out of meetings with multiple salespeople from multiple companies. They're subjected to the standard format of getting formalities out the way, answering standard questions, and then listening to the pitch. Maybe there'll be a bit of spicy objection handling if they're lucky, followed by a killer close for the finale. It gets a little tiresome. Out of the blue, one of the salespeople swoops in with a witty one liner, a touch of self-deprecation or a perfectly timed comeback. Suddenly, Client X is enjoying the meeting a little more.

In keeping with the idea of dropping your polite, polished sales alter ego and letting your personality spill out - don't be scared to be funny with your clients. Think of a tried and tested hilarious anecdote and share it in meetings if you're not blessed with being quick off the draw. Clients aren't fussy, honestly. Use a little humour to lighten the meeting and they'll remember you more fondly than your poker-faced competitors.

But what if you're not funny, you say? We'll I've been there... to the point I had to slowly repeat my joke back to a client in a last-ditch attempt to gain understanding. It was awkward obviously, but at least I tried.

Don't worry about ruining the relationship with a badly executed joke because you probably don't have a relationship to ruin yet. Sense check - this client isn't currently using you. You don't really have anything to differentiate your offering, other than a few beguiling USPs and "x number of years' experience." Nothing ground-breaking so far. You either risk a joke, make your client laugh and live happily ever after amid bonus and smiley faced emails, or you risk being forgotten about completely. Your call.

In real life

A sales guy asked about my plans for the weekend. I said, "quiet one, perhaps a movie." He replied, "Netflix and chill?" We laughed. It made me like him. It's that easy.

Disclaimer – I once worked with a chap who used humour as his main sales weapon. He got a lot of smiley faced emails and high yield accounts (romantically, he could probably joke his way into people's pants too). However, one day he misjudged his audience and cracked a joke about someone's ovaries. To an HR Manager, of all people. He never heard from that client again*.

Similarly, I don't think it's a bad idea to poke humour at your clients i.e. make fun of them, if you will. Sometimes we unconsciously cloak our clients in bubble wrap, place them on a pedestal and pop a crown on their head. We treat them like royalty because they're important people who can influence our income, success and career. So, we're polite and formal and god forbid we swear or act mildly inappropriately with them. Here's the thing – clients are people too and we should treat them as such. We shouldn't be looking up at them or worrying about what they'll think of us. Either they will like you and do business with you, or they won't. We should be able to be honest with them, have great conversations with them and have a laugh with them. In a romantic context, these things are highly sought after, so why would it be any different in business?

Date night

I once went on a date and unfortunately had a spot, which I did my best to conceal with makeup. I got to the bar and my date asked me what I wanted to drink. I gave him my order. He paused to ask if my spot wanted a drink too.

Perhaps don't make fun of your clients to the point where you offend them, but it's another great way to relax the relationship and bring in some natural ease. Granted, we're not all Kevin Bridges, but often you only have one shot, one opportunity to make an impression. You can choose to stand out, be yourself and gamble a little humour... or you can just keep sending rubbish emails, washing your mouth out with soap and being wholly unentertaining. What approach would be more fun for you, as well as your clients?

57

*Try and keep some sense of perspective please. This book won't be held responsible for you confusing "light hearted humour to win clients" with "sexually offensive remarks" that end with you on a blacklist.

Chapter 11 – War of the Robots

It's been predicted the world will be taken over by robots, and that a lot of jobs will be at risk. As proud patrons of one of the most hated professions, let's stand together as salespeople and prevent ourselves from becoming replaceable. How shall we do that? We'll make sure that being human remains an integral part of sales.

Frankly there are many salespeople who could already be mistaken for robots. You've probably worked with them, sat next to them, or perhaps unluckily been trained by them. They read the same scripts, in the same tone and sell exactly the same way as 90% of their peers. Our clients are on the receiving end of this siege. They are exposed to it day in, day out, and are starved of authentic pitches, fresh topics and genuine rapport. Your mission as a salesperson of today, is to break through the dusty, lacklustre habits of the industry and offer your clients a spark of individuality.

Let your quirks shine through your synthetic sales shell. Stop selling the same way everyone else does. Work out what makes you different. What is it that makes you likeable? Good to work with? Why should anyone buy from you vs. all your competitors? And most importantly, how are you going to get this across to your clients?

Just as we all want to date decent, funny, interesting, 10/10s - clients want to do business with great people. They want to believe their business matters and that they're in the hands of a human being who cares. They should never feel that they're only a company name in a database, with a forecasted value and a number of days lapsed prompting someone to call them. A robot could memorise an opener and rhyme off a script if we let it. A computer can send out mass, mail merged emails with zero personality. That's not adding value. That's not holding conversations. Clients have come to expect this though, and we've come to settle for it as the definition of "sales."

It's hard for us to prove we're the people worth doing business with. It's harder than it's ever been for us to overcome our industry stereotype, our client's guardedness and our endless number of competitors. If we all sound the same as each other, how can we expect anyone to tell us apart? How many millions of sales men and women with great potential, had their careers cut short, because they were never able to make it past the first ten seconds on the phone?

In real life

A long time ago I worked on the checkouts of a major retailer, scanning barcodes and packing bags. There was of course an aspect of sales in this too. The aim was to sign up as many customers as possible to the loyalty card. We all know loyalty cardholders spend an average of 4 times more than those without, plus the addition of their customer profile – location, income, spending habits etc. – enhances the effectiveness of targeted promotional activity. There was a weekly prize for the checkout girl who signed up the highest number of cards. This would be something along the lines of a packet of cigarettes or a £3 bottle of Lambrini, but the incentives worked.

*One day I'd brought my first real leather bag into work
and accidentally spilled a bottle of turps on it. Of course, it
was ruined. However, that day I told every customer who
passed through my till the story and asked for their
advice. Not a traditional sales technique you'll agree, but
somehow, that day I signed up a record number to our
loyalty scheme.*

Why did a ruined leather bag equal success? A few
reasons:

- It was different. How many times in your life have
  you ever passed through a checkout and been
  quizzed on your knowledge of turps vs. leather?
- It created engagement. I shared something about
  myself (my love for that bag) and invited
  participation. They became involved.
- We laughed. I do believe most people are quite
  nice once you have broken down the guarded
  exterior they reserve for the public domain. With
  this funny little scenario, the customers and I
  bonded over the predicament.
- Quite honestly, they probably felt a bit sorry for
  me. I didn't go in for the hard sell but who was
  honestly going to refuse to put their details on a
  form and make my day a bit better. A true soft
  touch.

If you can, find a way to instantly display something
personable about yourself. Use it cut through your client's
defences. Even if every morning you come in and pick a
topic for the day e.g. you got locked out the house, you
got caught in the rain and are sitting at your desk like a

drowned rat, there's a hole in your shoe (I've used all of these), say something a human would say to start off the call. If this is the first thing your sales interactions open with, you'll be making it clear you're not one of the robots. You'll get human replies - empathy, perhaps a shared tale of breaking into your own home, follow up questions. You're defying the dark side and embarking on a subject that might pave the way to a genuine conversation.

It's hard to like someone who has their guard up. Think about it - you never really start to like your clients until they warm up later in the process and begin to let their personalities peer through. So of course, it's awkward, intimidating and a little strange to be carelessly throwing chat and stories at a stranger who is ice cold. Half the time clients clam up as soon as they hear your job title and company. They brace themselves for what they think is coming next. Don't let yourself contribute to their anticipation of another terrible sales call. Throw in a curve ball and present them with qualities they didn't see coming. We are the professionals after all; we're paid not to need a minute in the microwave. We are the ones who have mastered likeability, open questioning and the skills to get our clients to unravel.

In real life

I used to keep an excel tracker with all my target accounts on it. It contained standard data such as contact information, account type, decision maker, etc. But it had a special column at the end called 'Misc.' In this column would be details of their family, their upcoming holidays, what sports they followed or the book they were reading. Despite its title, this was secretly the most important column of all. This was where I would retain and collate personal material I could use every time I spoke to them. I didn't call and say, "Hi, can I have your business please?" I'd call and say, "Have you finished the book yet?" or "Did you get a tan in Portugal?"

Aim to get to the point where every time you call a client, you can pull out a topic that's especially tailored to them. It can take a while to build the information up, but if you get just one tiny scrap on each attempt, you'll have something to work with next time. Stop interpreting the 'research' part of the sales model as analysing past spending habits, conversion rates and company organograms. Start learning the names of your target clients' kids* instead. You're more likely to get a bite if you surprise them with a novel approach and an affirmation that you're not another sales robot.

*don't focus on the kids exclusively, that could be creepy.

Chapter 12 - Personal Brand

In this day and age, it wouldn't be a very relevant sales guide, if there wasn't the mention of personal brand. Your personal brand isn't about the company you work for or the products you sell. Your personal brand is solely about the image you present to your clients, colleagues and network.

Think about your favourite footballer, YouTuber, president or celebrity. We warm to these people from a distance because they let their personalities shine in everything they do. We read their stories in magazines. We learn about their likes and dislikes from interviews, and get glimpses of where they go and how they spend their time on social media. We like them because we feel like we know them. This is the essence of likeability. You don't even need to be in the same room as someone to create it. This should be the way you approach the creation of your personal brand.

In sales, we can literally be headhunted for our personal brand – our reputation and relationships are our greatest assets. Clients buy from people, not companies. They may use a 'company' as their supplier but if they don't like the person they're dealing with, that business won't be there for long. Often they will continue to work with the same salesperson over several career moves because it's the individual that influences the service they get, more than who's employing them. The client has decided they like them, trust them, and feel like they know them.

If you have a strong personal brand and enviable client relationships, you will always have options on the job market. Obviously, billings are important too, but that's actually a by-product of your ability to leverage likeability to win accounts. What's more, very few sales jobs exclude "developing new business" from the job spec, so you're going to be expected to do this wherever you go. If you're equipped to create viable connections with new clients quickly, you'll have the prowess you need to be successful in any new role.

I don't believe some people are made for sales and other aren't. I've watched softly spoken wallflowers, and suited and booted sharks, veterans and naïve new starts (who don't know what a ride they're in for), and all these people have been hugely effective at what they do. Salespeople don't have to fit a common mould. Not anymore. Because no matter what company they worked for or what product they were selling, these salespeople found a way to get clients to like them, and that aspect of sales will never become outdated.

So always be investing in your personal brand. Be nice to everyone you encounter from the receptionist to the CEO. Treat your colleagues and boss and clients with the respect they deserve. Try and date all of them. Be one of the nice guys, the good guys, and let your reputation take you places. We may work in an infamous industry, we but certainly don't have to be villains.

Final date night

Things may not have worked out with me and the guys mentioned in this book. However, none of them were bad people. A lot of them were amazing actually, and despite the fact I'm "no longer working with them," there are a few I wouldn't hesitate to recommend. Clients don't last forever either. Sometimes accounts dwindle or people move on. Even with the best will in the world, sometimes things don't work out. This can be said of any type of relationship.

However, the very best you can hope for is:

- *a good time while you're together*
- *that you're remembered fondly*
- *that they'll happily distribute your business cards to other interested parties*

Conclusion

There's a lot we can learn from the world of dating. There are so many schools of thought on developing likeability and it's astonishing we rarely factor this into our sales strategy. Yes – of course you have to be strong on delivery too, however you'll never get to demonstrate that part of your game if no one likes you enough to give you a shot.

In an increasingly impersonal age, strive to put the human connection back into your work. Use these techniques on gatekeepers, at networking events, in the office, in your personal life too, and see where you can deepen connections and add more value. Of course, some traditional models and techniques will always have their place in the sales process. Once you get your relationships going, you can question funnel the fuck out them and apply all the kinky conversation ratios you like. However, in the meantime, work at treating your clients like people again, and maybe they'll start to treat you like a person back.

Saying you work in sales is no longer the cool, cigar smoking, rolodex scrolling, typecast it used to be. In fact, many salespeople face judgement and negativity due to the connotations of our job. Perhaps the industry didn't upgrade and adapt its practices as quickly as the client landscape changed, leaving us holding our phones looking outdated and seedy.

But if we can start to shift our mindset back to focussing on the real connections between clients and salespeople, on trust and openness, and being ourselves, then hopefully it will be a step in the right direction.

We are not sea turtles. Humans naturally seek people to relate to and if you can make this the foundation of your approach with clients, you'll have a long, prosperous and gratifying time in sales.

Now get grafting, and go date your clients.

Acronyms

KPI	-	Key performance indicator
SLA	-	Service level agreement
BAU	-	Business as usual
DMC	-	Deep meaningful conversation
AWOL	-	Absent without leave
MIA	-	Missing in action
POV	-	Point of view
IM	-	Instant message
DM	-	Direct message
USP	-	Unique selling point

About the Author

This book was self-published so I'd find it silly to write this part in traditional third person.

I've been selling for almost as long as I've been dating. My first sales job was offering ice-cream at the intermission breaks in our local theatre. After that, I moved onto a part-time job in a DIY chain where I learned to design and sell kitchens, bathrooms and fitted bedrooms. I still remember the sales model they used to train us. It was called MUSIC. God only knows who came up with that, but I cut my teeth on it anyway.

Finally, I moved on to what many regard as the hardest sales job of all - selling people (also known as recruitment). After years of working with top performers and being one of them, I realised that none of our success came from the models and techniques and tricks we'd been taught. It was purely because we were good with people.

Something in the sales culture was wrong. We were meant to treat clients like ATMs, business like transactions and KPIs like the bible. Everything was focused on call numbers, meeting frequency, average invoice values and the ££££s on the board at the end of the month.

So, I wrote this book to realign the emphasis on the people involved, and the relationships we develop with them, rather than cold hard figures we often get carried away with. How we treat people is, in my opinion, what sets apart good salespeople from great ones.

I may not have always had the best product or cheapest deal, or even the greatest level of service, but because my clients liked dealing with me, they gave me business. They even told other people to give me business.

I've always found there are a lot of parallels between sales and dating, plus it's nice to turn those odd encounters into something useful. Hopefully this book will serve two purposes:

1. to bring the human element back into sales
2. to remind everyone that in sales, and in life, the basis of any relationship starts with authentic communication

If you enjoyed this book, please share it with colleagues and connections, or leave a nice review. I'm a millennial after all, so appreciate these things.

Thanks for reading.

Best wishes,

Lauren

Find me on LinkedIn.

#dateyourclients

First Reactions

Me, tentatively declaring...

''I'm going to write a book.''

My Mum

*gushes with

uninhibited/unrelenting/unbounded/wholehearted

praise and positivity

the way only a mother can do when

her child announces an idea*

My Flatmate (& best friend of 20 years)

*glances over to look at me briefly while still watching
Teen Moms*

"Well yeah, isn't that what you're destined to do?"

Printed in Great Britain
by Amazon